MW00651236

MAKE
The Numbers,

Don't CHASE
The Numbers!

How to efficiently manage
and balance the details of
a complex business

Mark Payne

Penworth Publishing
Humble, Texas

www.MakeTheNumbers.com

Published by
Penworth Publishing
6942 FM 1960 East, #152
Humble, Texas 77346
www.penworth.com

ISBN: 978-0-97531-396-1

Printed in the United States of America

Library of Congress Cataloging-in-Publication Data
Payne, Mark
Make the Numbers, Don't Chase the Numbers:
efficiently manage and balance the details of a complex business/business/
operations / Mark Payne
p.cm. - (Make the Numbers series)
ISBN 978-0-97531-396-1
1. Books - Business - Handbooks, manuals, etc. 2. Operations industries
and trade - Handbooks, manuals, etc. 3. Procedures - Handbooks,
manuals, etc. 4. Inventory Control - Handbooks, manuals, etc. I. Title:
Make the Numbers, Don't Chase the Numbers II. Payne, Mark
III. Title.I.Series.
LCCN 2006937247

*This book is available for bulk purchases. For information,
go to www.MakeTheNumbers.com.*

www.MakeTheNumbers.com

This book is dedicated to my parents.

Acknowledgment

A special thanks to Jim Clayton for his contributions and to Symphony-Metreo Corporation for developing a software solution that supports the Make The Numbers Approach.

Matthew 22:37-39

www.MakeTheNumbers.com

www.MakeTheNumbers.com

Table of Contents

Introduction .... Page 1 - 3

Chapter 1: The Problem .... Page 4 - 25

Chapter 2: The Solution .... Page 26 - 57

Chapter 3: Implementation of MTNA .... Page 58 - 79

Chapter 4: Benefits of MTNA .... Page 80 - 95

Chapter 5: Conclusion .... Page 96 - 97

Epilogue .... Page 98 - 99

Index .... Page 100 - 107

"Make the Numbers, Don't Chase the Numbers" Expanded Outline:

CHAPTER 1: The Problem
I. Plans do not align with other departmental groups
- Typical annual planning exercise

II. Business does not have a cross-departmental problem solving framework to adjust to the realities of the marketplace
- Reality hits and the departments manage from their own point of view
- Departments communicate with each other through aggregated data
- Departments work at different levels of information to run the business; when reality hits - only top-down approach is applied

III. Departments work in silos and chase the numbers which sub-optimizes the entire enterprise
- Examples of departments running in silos that sub-optimize the entire enterprise

CHAPTER 2: The Solution
I. Theoretical Answer
- We need plans to be aligned and synchronized across departments
- We need a framework that immediately shows the cross-departmental impact of any change or adjustment
- Thus, getting the business out of the "silo mode"

II. MTNA (Make The Numbers Approach)
- The Level that Matters
- The Objective and Measures
- MTNA Gameboard flow
- Out of Bounds Conditions
- Multi-dimensional Roll Up of the MTNA Gameboard

CHAPTER 3: Implementation of MTNA

I.   Assess current business model and organization
II. Change Organization
  ▪ Add the Sales & Operations Planning group between the Demand and Supply organizations
III. Set up the MTNA Gameboard for all SKUs
IV. Educate the Demand and Supply organizations on how to be a part of MTNA
V.   Implement the system that supports MTNA

CHAPTER 4: Benefits of MTNA

I.   Business is working off one set of Operational Numbers
  ▪ Unit Plan is completed - no need to make up your own forecast or set of numbers
II. The production signal is managed and smoothed
  ▪ Factories and Suppliers get a smoother signal across time that increases their predictability and profitability
III. Departments will work together to proactively balance the demand and supply picture
  ▪ The departments get out of passing data and solving problems one variable at a time
IV. Other benefits of MTNA
  ▪ Allows top-down management to drive bottoms-up execution
  ▪ MTNA can be run with a flat organizational structure
  ▪ Merger and Acquisitions can be done in a different and more efficient way

CHAPTER 5: Conclusion

iv

ABOUT THE AUTHOR
Mark Payne

Mark Payne is a native of Texas who enjoyed growing up in the Lone Star State. He was the child of a small business owner who encouraged him to participate in their family owned enterprise during his teen age years. In addition, by the time he was seventeen, Mark had obtained his single engine pilot's license, just like his Dad.

Mark received a BBA degree from Baylor University, where he majored in Quantitative Business Analysis. Following graduation, Mark's first job was working for Uncle Ben's Rice, an M&M Mars Company, as a Plant Scheduler. That initial job helped launch his career in the consumer packaged goods industry. Mark's next role at Uncle Ben's Rice was in the Sales department. It was at this juncture that he began forming his opinion about how demand organizations and supply organizations should communicate with each other.

Later, he further developed and refined his ideas in a larger scale at Compaq, where he managed the operations of a $12 billion section of that company. While at Compaq, Mark also became involved in merger and acquisitions activities. He then decided to work with Symphony-Metreo for the next six months to develop a software solution for the consumer packaged goods sector. Next, Mark proceeded to Polaroid as Vice President of Operations. During his tenure there, Mark helped bring Polaroid out of bankruptcy and into profitability.

Next, he went to work for Linksys as Vice President of Worldwide Operations and began driving their business model with his proven methodology.

Introduction

Does the business environment that you participate in daily *"make the numbers or chase the numbers?"*

Have you written or received a memo making the following announcement in your business?

> **"All departments must cut their budgets by 10% to make the quarterly or annual business plan."**

In response, every department looks at where they are spending their money and must trade-off or *"give up"* something to meet the new budget targets. Business activities like travel, advertising, product promotions, purchases, and new hires, are all deferred to another time.

If the numbers are still short of expectations, the business typically decides that more drastic measures are required.

The business can try to *"stuff"* the market with unwanted products. Layoffs or restructuring could be required to close the gap and make the numbers that were promised to the shareholders or owners.

The direction to adjust the business comes from the *"top-down"* because there is a financial gap that needs to be closed. Usually the gap is created by demand and/or supply issues. A desired financial result is pushed down through the organization, and the details are forced to match the desired result. Unfortunately, the details can never be aligned because there are too many variables to realistically balance the business at any one point in time.

This *"chasing the numbers"* approach of forcing a *"top-down"* answer into the detailed work stream of a business is a sub-optimal and reactive way to run a business. Employees who work at a detailed level say things like, *"The people at the top do not have a clue."* In most cases, they are correct. Morale, employee productivity, and the business all suffer in this type of environment. However, there is a better way to *"Make The Numbers!"*

Over the last fifteen years, I have developed and taught a simple structure and process that allows all departments in a business to work together to proactively and efficiently control the performance and results of the business every day.

 KEY INFO! **I call this process MTNA** *(Make The Numbers Approach)*

Why, you ask, do I need to read another book on business process and organization? Because this concept really will change the way you think about your business. You will be able to implement MTNA in your business, and you will change your business environment into an efficient, well-organized, profit-making enterprise. MTNA will help every business get out of the *"chase the numbers"* mode of operation.

This *"how to"* book is set up to be an efficient use of your time. I will define the business problem; then move quickly into the solution, which is MTNA. After you understand how MTNA works, I will explain how to implement it in your business. I will end the book by summarizing the benefits and results MTNA brings to those who implement it fully.

Make the Numbers, Don't Chase the Numbers!

How to efficiently manage and balance the details of a complex business.

What kind of businesses can benefit from this proven methodology? MTNA is designed for businesses that have a large product offering and volume. The business can either produce or buy the product it offers to the marketplace. If your business offers less than 200 items or does not turn the items (i.e. your business makes and sells one widget per year), MTNA will not help your business model as much. MTNA works better and benefits a more complex high volume company that has become inefficient and slow in making decisions.

"How do you get a cork out of an empty wine bottle without breaking the bottle or the cork?"

THE PROBLEM

Have you ever been given the full demonstration of trying to get a cork out of a wine bottle without, of course, breaking the bottle or the cork? First, you drink the wine and empty the bottle. Second, you push the cork back into the empty bottle of wine. This is not an easy task. After a few strong pushes with your thumbs, the cork finally finds its way to the bottom of the bottle. Then, the person demonstrating the trick says, *"now that you have the cork in the bottle, get it out!"*

In business we push the cork in the bottle by:

1. Making plans that don't align to other departmental groups.
2. Not having a cross-departmental problem solving frame-work to adjust to the realities of the marketplace.
   * Leadership is actually flying blind and making decisions that are then forced down through the business; the "top-down make the details match" drill that never works.

Thus leaving

3. Departments to their own devises *(or silos)* to do what they can to *"chase the numbers."*

Allow me to illustrate these problems with real world examples:

Problem #1
Plans Don't Align to Other Departmental Groups.

Let's start with the origins of the annual business plan. How does it come into existence? Here is the typical drill. For most companies the annual planning process starts in the summer and ends in December. Designing the annual business plan is a long, exhausting process that usually starts with an overriding business strategy that drives the Marketing department to forecast next year's product portfolio. The Sales department develops quotas for the current and future product portfolio. Production and purchasing plans are made; inventory and cash are projected; expenses rolled up, and on and on. All of these numbers pour in from different groups based on the responsibilities of each department and decidedly from their individual perspectives. There is usually a small planning group that is responsible for collecting the cross-departmental information and driving the planning process.

After a meeting or two, all the departments go to work creating their piece of next year's plan from the bottom-up.

A typical first pass at the annual plan looks something like this: The Marketing team adds fifty new products to the product portfolio to meet the projected growth within the market-place. Production and procurement costs per product stay flat versus last year. The Sales department believes it will sell less than the market is growing because the Sales department is not sure how the new products will perform, and the current product portfolio needs a lower cost/price to compete in the marketplace. All the administrative departments will need to increase their budgets to implement automated systems for greater efficiencies.

The departments turn in their numbers, and the Finance team tallies the results. And guess what happens next... *the plan is short of expectations.* Have you ever heard of an annual plan being blessed on the first try? In some awkward but humorous occasions the Leadership of the company is left scratching its head. They say things like, *"How can our expenses be going up this dramatically while our sales remain flat in a growing market?"* Good question.

The reality is that the annual business plan is not a plan at all. Businesses do not run an annual planning process that optimizes business results against the real marketplace. The annual planning process is actually a negotiation process. Most numbers are biased from the start to protect the turf of each department. In reality, each department has already tainted the numbers by its own viewpoint, so much so that the departments are never in sync with each other. What started out as a bottom-up planning drill that would line up the product details and departments, turns into a top-down *"go get this number and make the details work"* negotiation exercise that sub-optimizes the overall business.

The dance is always the same. The numbers are pulled up from the bottom, and the numbers are predictably short of expectations. Then, the over-inflated numbers come from the Leadership at the top, and the product details at the bottom are forced to match. Everyone involved runs out of time because nobody can reconcile the product details at the bottom. The end of the planning timeline arrives, and the department heads are forced to compromise, and nothing optimal remains for anyone.

So, what happens next? Time's up, pencils down, and the negotiation is over. The annual plan gets approved and individual performance measures are set for everyone to meet, from the Leadership all the way down to the Teams. Departments line up behind their specific level of information, which, of course, does not reconcile with any other department in the business.

**CORK IN THE BOTTLE
SUMMARY OF PROBLEM #1:**

The department plans do not align because the numbers were never real in the first place.

Questions For Your Annual Business Planning Process

(I asked these questions to a group of Leaders within the company. *I've included the answers I received.)

1) How long does your product detail planning process reach out into time, and what time frame do you send your suppliers?

   Answer I received - "One year for both."

2) Does the planning time horizon roll on, or does it stop at the end of the year?

   Answer I received - "Stops at the end of the year."

3) How long is your longest lead-time item within your product bill-of-materials?

   Answer I received - "Two years."

4) Does your longest lead-time item's time-horizon exceed your detailed planning time-horizon at any part during the year?

   Answer I received - "Obviously yes. And, next year's plan will be completed in November."

5) So, who is really deciding how much to make and sell for next year and beyond?

   Answer I received - "Someone in the Purchasing department must be making volume commitments to our suppliers."

KEY INFO! WHO REALLY CONTROLS YOUR BUSINESS?

Answer: The people who work at the bottom of the organization and actually touch the details.

Problem #2
Companies do not have a cross-departmental problem solving framework to adjust to reality.

Even if the plan were perfectly assembled and all departmental areas of the business were aligned and in-sync *(big assumption!)*, the day after the plan is approved, reality hits.

All of the assumptions and all of the irrelevant trade-offs become wasted efforts because the environment in which a business operates does not remain static long enough for the business to meet projected numbers that were flawed to begin with. Competition, suppliers, customers, product forecasts, new product performance, factory execution, and the weather are not one hundred percent predictable. Unfortunately, all businesses must deal with all of these variables and more at the same time. Each variable has a different effect on a business. When all these variables are mixed together, the business must manage itself in an environment that is downright unpredictable and ever changing.

As the realities of the market reveal themselves each week, all departments are forced to make trade-offs and adjust the business. Overselling or underselling the product forecasts, competitor price moves, losing a key customer, bad weather, key suppliers going out of business, and the fickle marketplace all put pressure on a business to react. Most businesses do not have a problem solving framework to manage this reality. All departments typically manage the business from their own points of view.

Regardless, departments need to communicate with each other to adjust the business to the ever-changing realities. Because businesses lack a cross-departmental problem solving framework at a detailed level, departments aggregate business results to communicate with one another and report actual performance.

Let me give you an example:

The Sales department has committed to sell 100,000 units of product into the marketplace this month. The Manufacturing and Procurement departments have committed to make and place in inventory 100,000 units of the product to meet the overall sales forecast. There are three product families: **Product Family A** *(10% margin),* **Product Family B** *(20% margin),* and **Product Family C** *(50% margin).* The 100,000 unit sales forecast for the month was split by product family: 50,000 units forecasted for Product Family A, 30,000 units forecasted for Product Family B, and 20,000 units forecasted for Product Family C. Manufacturing and Procurement departments produced the exact amount of product required to match the product family forecast.

The actual sales for the month came in at 110,000 units for all product families combined. Did the business achieve its financial goals? If you aggregate the product families, it appears the Sales department did exceed the sales forecast by 10,000 units this month. If you are asking me to reveal the product family level sales details for the month, your instincts are sharp.

The actual sales for the month by product family came in at the following:

- ◆ **Product Family A** sold 80,000 units vs. 50,000 forecasted
  (10% margin)
- ◆ **Product Family B** sold 25,000 units vs. 30,000 forecasted
  (20% margin)
- ◆ **Product Family C** sold 5,000 units vs. 20,000 forecasted
  (50% margin)

Did you remember the margin percentages for each product family? The reality in the marketplace was different from what was forecasted. The market purchased more of the low margin Product Family A versus the higher margin Product Families B and C.

Let me repeat the question:
> Did the business achieve its financial goals?
> *Answer:* No.

Remember that the Manufacturing and Procurement departments made the exact amount of product family inventory required to meet the product family sales forecast. This means that the business has too much inventory for high margin Product Families B and C and too little inventory for low margin Product Family A.

The irony is that the Manufacturing and Procurement departments are probably trying to expedite raw materials at any cost to make more of the 10% margin Product Family A, while high margin Product Families B and C take up cash and space in the warehouse.

THE REALITY:
Nothing goes according to plan!

Because businesses lack a common problem solving framework, departments, leadership, leaders, and teams all look at the business at different levels of information. Departments will have a tendency to aggregate their data to communicate their results and justify their trade offs and actions. The most dangerous way to manage a business is by solely viewing aggregated results. Data aggregation is an easier way to look at and explain the business; however, data aggregation will minimize the effect reality has on the business. In the example above, what if the business paid the Sales group bonuses based on the actual 110,000 unit sales achieved for the month? If the business environment allows the majority of the departments to manage the business at high levels in the information hierarchies, the business will waste tons of money. Reality will run over the business because the practice of managing the business at aggregated information levels hides the details of what is causing the problems. In the example, the marketplace purchased a different product family mix from what the sales forecast assumed. So, fix the product family sales mix problem. Don't pay bonuses for exceeding the sales forecast by 10,000 units.

The old saying is true: *The devil is in the details.* My new saying: *Don't wish for results. Manage the details; roll up the results.*

Another phenomenon of data aggregation is that there is a *"spinning and tainting"* of the numbers as they are presented to Leaders, to benefit the group presenting. Departments and individuals are always trying to justify their value within the business. The Leadership typically does not have visibility to the details at the bottom of the data hierarchies. Thus, Leadership is flying blind and trusting the interpretation of the information given to them by the Leaders and Teams.

As departments stay away from managing the details with other departments, the business reacts to reality from the top-down and the details cannot be reconciled. Thus, the decisions and direction coming from the top-down cannot be executed.

Let me give you a departmental example of how businesses lack a common problem solving framework to adjust to reality.

A large competitor lowers pricing, and consumer demand plummets across the most profitable line of products.

Competition does not sit still for anyone. Last quarter, a competitor lowered its price, and its action is making the company's most profitable product line decline by 50%. The business purchases this product line from multiple suppliers, so the finished goods inventory is rising fast. The business is halfway through the current quarter and cannot afford to lower the price in order to chase the competition. However, the business needs the revenue and profits from the troubled product line to maintain the annual plan performance targets.

So, how do the major departments typically react when they hear the shocking news of the competitor's price move?

The Leadership of the company tasks Marketing to come up with a new product portfolio that will make up the margin and revenue difference. The Leadership also tasks Finance to come up with a new business model, after Marketing defines the new product strategy. The Leadership will request a short-term and long-term solution immediately.

The Sales department is screaming to lower the price because sales of the product line are being beaten in the marketplace. The Sales group is signaling risk to the revenue plan because product sales will not be able to meet the projected revenue numbers due to the competitor's effect on the marketplace.

Manufacturing and Procurement departments are locked into their supplier contracts. If the overall volumes are going down, then the costs per unit will be going up. The suppliers will be pressuring the business to raise prices, not lower them.

The Finance department is looking at the numbers because it was counting on normal revenue and margin figures. Finance is now of the opinion that big layoffs are coming.

Two weeks later:

Marketing and Finance put together high-level plans that remix the product offering. This plan has been designed at a top level in the product hierarchy, and all of the details have been assumed to be workable. Sales, Manufacturing, and Procurement are not sure what the answer is because the high-level plan does not get low enough into the product hierarchy to be meaningful to their current plans. Therefore, Sales, Manufacturing, and Procurement departments attempt to align the details to the higher level plan assumptions.

COMMENTARY: Different departments solve business problems at different hierarchy levels of time, measures, geography, and product. While some groups think they have the solution in hand, other groups are left bridging the gap and filling in the details - a reaction that results in chaos and poor business execution.

A new approach is needed to manage the details and roll up the results in each department's view; one that will adjust to reality with precision and control.

Hint: MTNA

CORK IN THE BOTTLE
SUMMARY OF PROBLEM #2:

The business does not have a common problem solving framework to roll up the details and manage reality; only "top-down make the details work" aggregated approach.

Problem #3

Departments are left to their own devises to "Chase the Numbers" from their "silo" perspective.

The plan details by department do not align to other functions, and there is no problem solving framework for all departments to work the details together to manage reality. So, the Leaders and Teams in each department chase the numbers from their perspective in the business. They do not anticipate or coordinate with other departments to solve the problems; *the departments just react using their own data, systems, and spreadsheets.* Most of the time the departments unknowingly work against each other by trying to optimize their own section of the business while sub-optimizing the entire business. It becomes every man or department for itself, and silos within the business run at full strength.

"Chasing the Numbers"
Business Examples – Silos

I am going to share with you some examples of changes that have happened to businesses and how most of the departments deal with the reality that faces them. Later, in Chapter 2, *The Solution,* you will learn a better way to manage the details and reality in what I like to call MTNA *(Make the Numbers Approach).* But for now, enjoy watching these departments *"Chase the Numbers."*

Silo Example #1
New product launch is delayed by five weeks.

The Marketing group planned for a new family of products that the company produces to be available at the end of the month. The business got the news on the third day of the month that the new product family would be delayed for five weeks due to an engineering delay. The original business plan had all of the old products winding down and going away at the end of this month. The entire company was on the same page and was planning to market, sell, and produce the new products to meet the marketplace demands and make an orderly transition.

So, how do the major departments typically react when they hear the surprising news about the delay?

The Leadership of the company will throw money and resources at the engineering department to correct the problem. The Leadership wants to make the five-week delay shrink to a two-week delay. They will not know the probability of success for another two weeks.

The Marketing department could not push off the advertising campaign because Marketing was within its lead-times. This situation was going to be one of those *"advertise first, product follows later"* launches.

The Sales department delays the new product launch meetings and presentations to their customers and keeps on driving to its quarterly quota number by continuing to sell the old product family. The Sales group will reschedule the new product launch meetings when it sees new product inventory in the warehouse.

Manufacturing and Procurement departments begin to make their production and purchasing adjustments immediately. Manufacturing begins to crank up and produce the old product family. Manufacturing cannot let the factory sit idle. So, Manufacturing pays to expedite eight-week's worth of raw materials just in case there is another delay.

The Finance department is looking at the numbers, and it was counting on the new product family to drive a higher revenue and margin number. Finance is drafting a note to all departments asking them to cut back on all expenses until the business gets through this crisis.

Two weeks later:
Leadership announces that the engineering problem has

been solved. The business can begin producing the new product family immediately. The business is currently only one week behind schedule.

> **COMMENTARY:** Every department came up with a logical solution that made complete sense to each group. This form of decision making is called *"silo-based"* decision making. The first department or departmental head's reaction is to optimize his or her area of responsibility, because that is what he or she can control. The bigger picture is an afterthought. Most Leaders and Teams in a business cannot see the entire business complexity and make the necessary trade-offs because a process does not exist to optimize the entire business.

Silo Example #2
Product demand exceeds wildest expectations as demand rises 200% over the sales forecast this month.

The Marketing team has hit the sweet spot and the Sales team is on fire. One of the premium products is selling fast, and the business has only one week of finished goods inventory across the entire globe. Many sales regions are stocking out and are looking for information to set customers' expectations. The Manufacturing and Procurement departments are working to close the gap. So, how do the major departments typically react when they hear the exciting news about the hot seller?

The Leadership of the company praises the Marketing and Sales groups for superb execution in the marketplace, and then asks the Manufacturing and Procurement groups when they can cover the backorders on the books.

Marketing and Sales departments continue to promote and sell the product hard. They are exceeding their targeted numbers easily. All future sales orders are going directly into backorder status.

Manufacturing and Procurement departments are scrambling to get parts and create capacity to produce as much of the hot seller as possible. Manufacturing and Procurement groups do not want to be known as the *"Sales Prevention"* departments. So, they expedite at any cost to get the necessary extra capacity and parts to satisfy demand and to increase market-share.

The Finance department is optimistically counting the money. The backorders are getting larger by the day, and if the business can ship the backorders before the quarter ends, the bottom line will be looking great.

Two weeks later:
Manufacturing and Procurement have expedited and will be able to cover only 75% of the current backlog. The balance of the current backlog and any new orders will not be shipped until next quarter. Therefore, customers have been over promised about product delivery, and maximum potential will not be obtained this quarter.

COMMENTARY: Businesses typically lack a way to proactively coordinate demand and supply at a detailed level. Businesses usually manage product forecasts and balance demand and supply at an aggregated level which makes overselling the sales forecast a reactive issue. Most businesses have more control over what they make or buy, versus control over the marketplace and order flow. This situation typically puts all the pressure on the supply chain to play catch-up at any cost when demand exceeds the forecast. Customer relationships are damaged because departments work within their own silo to solve issues, and no one is setting proper expectations with the sales force or customers, while Manufacturing and Procurement groups are overspending budgets to dig out of every overselling scenario.

CORK IN THE BOTTLE
SUMMARY OF PROBLEM #3:

Departments work in silos and "Chase the Numbers" which sub-optimizes the entire enterprise.

Cork in the bottle summary:

1. The department plans do not align. The numbers were never real in the first place.

2. The business does not have a cross-departmental problem solving framework to roll up the details and manage reality. They only use a *"top-down make the details work"* aggregated approach.

3. Departments work in silos and *"Chase the Numbers"* which sub-optimizes the entire enterprise.

All departments must work together with a common set of numbers, structure, and language to continuously optimize the details for the business. Businesses must have a common framework for threading the execution centers for changes and adjustments, because the marketplace can be unpredictable.

While reading these scenarios, did you see the wasted money and effort going out the door? Did the examples sound like the business you work in today? Did it seem like the problem happened, and then everybody reacted in an uncoordinated way? There was not one departmental solution that optimized the entire business because all the groups ran to their own silo to solve the problem.

I hope I got your mind working to solve the examples. From what perspective did you want to solve the problem? The truth is that there are infinite ways to solve these examples. There are many trade-offs that can be made in any business situation. The issue is that there is no structure or methodology to coordinate all the details across multiple departments to make the best, optimal trade. MTNA gives the business the structure and process required to proactively manage all departments at the detailed level that matters and deliver the financial profits that all companies look for.

MTNA affects:
- *Sales*
- *Marketing*
- *Revenue*
- *Manufacturing*
- *Procurement*
- *Finance*
- *Inventory*
- *Margin*

"Now that the cork is in the bottle, let's see how we can get it out without breaking the glass or the cork."

"If you believe having too much inventory is a bad thing and having too little inventory is a bad thing... there is only one place to be...

IN BALANCE!*"*

Mark Payne

THE SOLUTION

Imagine yourself sitting in a restaurant trying to figure out how to get a cork out of an empty bottle of wine. The first time I was given this demonstration, my mind went numb. I could not figure out how in the world to get that cork out without breaking the bottle or the cork. I thought the task was impossible. The reason someone thinks something is truly impossible is because that individual has never seen it done before. I needed something tangible to make me believe. I needed a hint! The person demonstrating the trick gave me a hint in a form of a riddle . . . *"The answer is in your lap. What is it?"*

Now I am going to give you a solution (not a hint) on how to solve the problems described in Chapter 1.

A Vision of the Ideal

MTNA is designed to allow a business to continuously plan, decide, and adjust the future demand and supply activity in order to maximize profit potential.

Theoretical Answer

◆ To **Make the Numbers** we need the plans to be real. We need the numbers aligned and synchronized across departments even though they come from different points of view.
◆ We need a framework that immediately shows the cross-departmental impact of any change and any adjustment.
◆ Instead of optimizing silos, we need to be optimizing the business.

At a high level, MTNA gets the business working on one set of numbers, aligns all departments, and creates a framework so that departments can optimize the future execution plans for the business. MTNA is a cross-departmental problem solving framework that requires the business to manage every SKU the company offers the marketplace. Each department views and plans the business from a fundamentally different point of view, so we must manage the details at the bottom of the product hierarchies and roll up one set of forward looking numbers to serve each of the departments. Alignment of all departments is achieved by finding the **common multi-dimensional denominators from which all departments pivot.** I call this the *"level that matters."* With the common hierarchal levels identified, we now need a framework at this level that synchronizes and aligns various departmental plans. This framework is the MTNA Gameboard.

Illustration #1 -
Manage the Details, Roll Up the Results into Multi-Dimensions

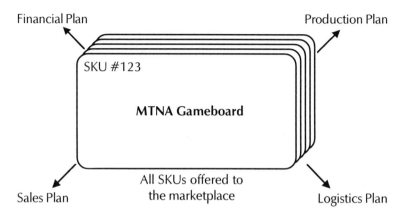

As I reveal the details to you in the following sections, MTNA allows us to see the impact of any change out in time *(forward looking)* to any departmental plan. To manage the business, we will manage the MTNA Gameboard and roll up the results to deliver the cross-departmental change to any future adjustment. The business will be planning and optimizing itself every week across a rolling time horizon of two years. All departments will proactively manage and control a bottom-up planning process that optimizes the demand and supply picture of the entire business. Now it's time to learn how to *"Make The Numbers."*

The *"Level That Matters"*

MTNA provides a common structure, set of numbers, and language for all departments to proactively solve demand and supply issues. A common structure and language are accomplished by selecting key demand and supply measures, while requiring all departments to use those measures in the same context. The focal point of MTNA becomes the product SKU *(Stock Keeping Unit)* level. When MTNA is running, the business will be **managed weekly** at the *"level that matters,"* with one set of numbers that all departments work with and view constantly. The finished goods level, or product SKU level, in the product hierarchy is the *"level that matters,"* and MTNA operates at this pivotal level. The product SKU is what manufacturing produces or supplies. The product SKU is what the marketplace purchases from the business *(the demand)*. At the product SKU level, information can be rolled up to Leadership via a product or geography hierarchy, or broken down into bill-of-material data for Manufacturing and Purchasing. Quite frankly, the product SKU level is the center of the universe for companies that offer products in the marketplace. All departmental reports and plans will pivot from the product SKU level.

Objective of MTNA
Control, balance, and optimize demand and supply continuously to maximize profit potential by managing products flowing into the marketplace at the *"level that matters."*

How MTNA works

The best way to explain the results of MTNA is to set up a MTNA Gameboard by SKU by week and let you see how the measures interact with real world examples as they move through time. Let me show you a methodology that is an efficient and effective way to balance demand and supply in your business and better control the results you promised to deliver.

Gameboard Measurement Set-Up *(by Product SKU by Week)*

The 7 measures that make up the gameboard are:
- ◆ Time
- ◆ Inventory
- ◆ Sales Forecast
- ◆ Production/Purchase
- ◆ Weeks-on-Hand
- ◆ Weeks-on-Hand Maximum
- ◆ Weeks-on-Hand Minimum

Each product SKU will have its own gameboard. The time horizon moves forward in weekly time frames using 104 weeks (two years). The MTNA Gameboard for each product will always stay 104 weeks long with each passing week... called the *"rolling 104 weeks"* time horizon.

One of the winning qualities of using MTNA is that the process will continuously yield an operational business plan of record. This plan can be used to update all other departmental plans to reflect current reality. This method avoids the problem of other departments making up their own reality over time.

Illustration #2 –

The MTNA Gameboard

Product SKU #123	Week 1	Week 2	Week 3	Week 4	Week 104
Inventory	400	300	500	400	400
Sales Forecast	100	100	100	100	100
Production/ Purchase	0	300	0	100	200
Weeks-on-Hand	4	3	5	4	4
Weeks-on-Hand Maximum	5	5	5	5	5
Weeks-on-Hand Minimum	3	3	3	3	3

Weeks-On-Hand Graph:

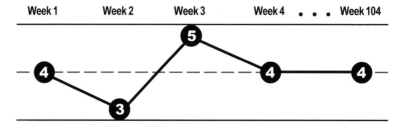

Week 1   Week 2   Week 3   Week 4   • • •   Week 104

MTNA Measure Definitions

Example: Product SKU #123

Time Horizon *(Known)* – The time horizon is defined by 104 weekly segments that roll forward continuously with each passing week. In the following examples, the time horizon is **not** reset to Week 1 after each passing week.

Inventory *(Known Number)* – The beginning inventory count of saleable Product #123's in finished goods owned by the company. The rest of the forward week's inventory can then be calculated.

> **Inventory - Sales + Production/Purchase = next week's inventory number.**

Week 1 Beginning Inventory – Week 1 Sales Forecast + Week 1 Production/Purchase = Week 2 Beginning Inventory

Sales Forecast *(Derived Number)* – The sales forecast of Product #123 by week until the end of the time horizon *(104 weeks)*.

Production/Purchase *(Derived Number to drive Weeks-on-Hand Measure)* – The production schedule or procurement schedule of Product #123 by week, until the end of the time horizon *(104 weeks)*.

Weeks-on-Hand *(Calculated)* – For every weekly time frame, a forward looking Weeks-on-Hand number is calculated based on how much saleable inventory will cover future sales.

For example, if in Week 5 the beginning inventory is 300 units and the sales forecast is 100 units per week in Week 5, Week 6, and Week 7, the 300 units in beginning inventory will cover three week's worth of **projected sales.** Every weekly time frame is calculated independently based on the beginning inventory and sales forecast. It is important to understand how the Weeks-on-Hand measure is calculated because it is **the key measure** used to balance the future demand and supply picture of the business.

Weeks-on-Hand Maximum and Minimum *(Derived and Adjusted)* - These numbers are the keys to driving the MTNA Gameboard. The Weeks-on-Hand settings will need to reflect the business model and execution capability by product SKU. The Weeks-on-Hand Maximum and Minimum measures are typically set up one time and then adjusted every 3 to 6 months to fine-tune the product SKU business model. The Weeks-on-Hand Maximum is the upper boundary of inventory that the business would want to keep. The Weeks-on-Hand Minimum is the lower boundary of inventory required to meet customer and service level expectations. For any future week, if the Weeks-on-Hand measure is above the Weeks-on-Hand Maximum or below the Weeks-on-Hand Minimum, that product SKU is "out of bounds" and requires a decision or adjustment. I will show you how to set the Weeks-on-Hand Maximum and Minimum measures later in the book, in Chapter 3, *Implementation of MTNA.*

MTNA Gameboard Time Flow

After all of the known and derived numbers have been entered onto the MTNA Gameboard, just like in real life, time rolls on. MTNA is proactive, not reactive. As time rolls onward and a week is completed, the MTNA picture changes by product SKU, and the business Leaders must decide to act or not to act.

"Don't be normal; be exceptional!"

. . . Mark Payne

Example MTNA Gameboard Problem #1
One product over time.

Let me take you through some basic examples that move forward in time for five weeks. Using illustration #3 for Product #123 as the original plan, the MTNA Gameboard moves onward through time.

Illustration #3 -

Product #123, Week 1 – *Original Plan*

Product SKU #123	Week 1	Week 2	Week 3	Week 4	Week 5
Inventory	400	300	500	400	400
Sales Forecast	100	100	100	100	100
Production/Purchase	0	300	0	100	200
Weeks-on-Hand	4	3	5	4	4
Weeks-on-Hand Maximum	5	5	5	5	5
Weeks-on-Hand Minimum	3	3	3	3	3

Weeks-On-Hand Graph:

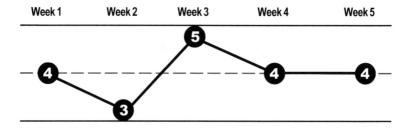

Time Rolls Onward: Week 2 *(Illustration #4)*

Actual sales for Product #123 was 50 units in Week 1 vs. 100 units forecasted. The differences are reflected in the forward looking inventory number over time. All future inventory numbers are increased by 50.

Illustration #4 –

New Picture of Product #123, Week 2

Product SKU #123	Week 2	Week 3	Week 4	Week 5	Week 6
Inventory	350	550	450	450	550
Sales Forecast	100	100	100	100	100
Production/ Purchase	300	0	100	200	100
Weeks-on-Hand	3.5	5.5	4.5	4.5	5.5
Weeks-on-Hand Maximum	5	5	5	5	5
Weeks-on-Hand Minimum	3	3	3	3	3

Weeks-On-Hand Graph:

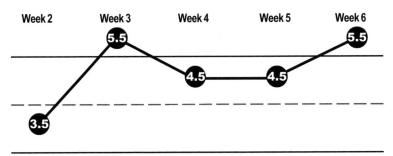

One week has gone by and the business is beginning Week 2. Product #123 has sold 50 units less than expected in Week 1. As a result, Week 3 and Week 6 *(and future weeks beyond)* are above the Weeks-on-Hand Maximum. Customers are not impacted because the business has plenty of finished goods inventory; however, the company is spending cash producing an item it does not need.

The point is that the business will actually see a specific product SKU go *"out of bounds"* and then must choose to deal with the issue in a specific way. When a company undersells a product, it can push out production or purchases to smooth future weeks outside lead times without doing any harm to customers or suppliers. In the case of Product #123, the decision was to leave the MTNA Gameboard alone because the Sales team thought they would have a good quarter and Week 1 was just an anomaly.

> ### Some key questions to ask about a SKU going "out of bounds" above the Weeks-on-Hand Maximum:
>
> *Is this a sales trend or an anomaly?*
>
> *Will sales rebound next week?*
>
> *When do we need to make a decision to cut back on production and supply?*
>
> *If we cut production or supply, how will the cut affect the factory and/or suppliers?*

Time Rolls Onward: Week 3 *(Illustration #5)*

Actual sales for Product #123 was 200 units in Week 2, which made up for the sales shortfall in Week 1. The Sales group was right this time.

Illustration #5 -

New Picture of Product #123, Week 3

Product SKU #123	Week 3	Week 4	Week 5	Week 6	Week 7
Inventory	450	350	350	450	450
Sales Forecast	100	100	100	100	100
Production/ Purchase	0	100	200	100	100
Weeks-on-Hand	4.5	3.5	3.5	4.5	4.5
Weeks-on-Hand Maximum	5	5	5	5	5
Weeks-on-Hand Minimum	3	3	3	3	3

Weeks-On-Hand Graph:

Week 3	Week 4	Week 5	Week 6	Week 7

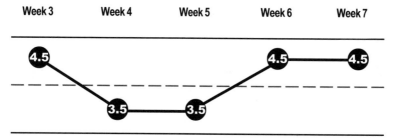

Another week has gone by and the business is beginning Week 3. The beginning inventory number for Product #123 is updated and now Product #123 is in balance and requires no action, because the Weeks-on-Hand measure is *"in bounds"* for all future weeks.

"Manage the details; roll up the results."

. . . Mark Payne

Time Rolls Onward: Week 4 *(Illustration #6)*

Actual sales for Product #123 was 200 units in Week 3. Sales are trending up.

Illustration #6 -

New Picture of Product #123, Week 4

Product SKU #123	Week 4	Week 5	Week 6	Week 7	Week 8
Inventory	250	250	350	350	350
Sales Forecast	100	100	100	100	100
Production/ Purchase	100	200	100	100	100
Weeks-on-Hand	2.5	2.5	3.5	3.5	3.5
Weeks-on-Hand Maximum	5	5	5	5	5
Weeks-on-Hand Minimum	3	3	3	3	3

Weeks-On-Hand Graph:

Week 4	Week 5	Week 6	Week 7	Week 8

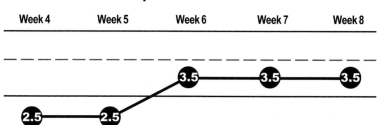

One more week has gone by, and the business is beginning Week 4. Product #123 has oversold two weeks in a row. Weeks-on-Hand for Week 4 and Week 5 (and future weeks beyond) are below the Weeks-on-Hand Minimum. Customers could be impacted in certain markets because Product #123 has oversold projections, and the business needs to decide what action to execute across all departments.

The point is that the business will see a specific product SKU go *"out of bounds"* and then must choose to deal with the issue in a specific way. When a company oversells a product, it needs to react in a coordinated way that optimizes the entire business. All the risks and costs need to be weighed before an action is selected. In the case of Product #123, the decision was to raise the forecast of Product #123. This decision includes raising the revenue and margin that financially matches the product.

Manufacturing and Procurement departments will start to procure the additional supply to produce enough to balance the MTNA Gameboard. The Manufacturing and Procurement departments will load the Production/Purchasing line with a **feasible plan** by the end of the week, so that all departments will have a clear picture in Week 5.

Some key questions to ask about a SKU going "out of bounds" below the Weeks-on-Hand Minimum:

Is this a sales trend or an anomaly?

Will sales continue to be higher than projected?

What is the cost for manufacturing and procurement to "pull in" and expedite production and supply?

When do we need to make a decision to increase production and supply?

If we add production or supply now, how will that affect the factory and/or suppliers?

When can we really catch up?

Time Rolls Onward: Week 5 *(Illustration #7)*

Actual sales for Product #123 was 200 units in Week 4, which were 100 units per week higher than originally forecasted. Sales are trending at 200 per week.

Illustration #7 -

New Picture of Product #123, Week 5

Product SKU #123	Week 5	Week 6	Week 7	Week 8	Week 9
Inventory	150	150	50	0	800
Sales Forecast	200	200	200	200	200
Production/ Purchase	200	100	150	1000	200
Weeks-on-Hand	0.75	0.75	0.25	0	4.0
Weeks-on-Hand Maximum	5	5	5	5	5
Weeks-on-Hand Minimum	3	3	3	3	3

Weeks-On-Hand Graph:

Week 5	Week 6	Week 7	Week 8	Week 9

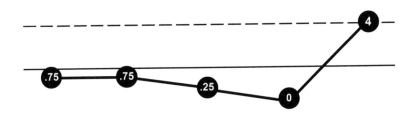

Another week has gone by and the business is beginning
Week 5. The Sales Forecast line has been updated along with
the Production/Purchase line. The best Manufacturing can do
is produce the amount required to balance the gameboard in
Week 8. Product #123 will stock out in Week 8 and be back
up to proper Weeks-on-Hand levels by the end of Week 9.
By now, the business knows what details to manage and when
the crisis will be over. Manufacturing and Procurement still
need to execute and the Sales department will need to set
the proper expectations with the customers. Time moves
onward.

> The weekly adjustments go on like a beating
> drum. The business is managing the details
> and making quicker decisions because
> MTNA provides a structure and logic
> behind each Product SKU that is *"out of*
> *bounds."*

Let's take a look at Week 1 – ***Original Plan*** chart versus actual ***Performance*** chart for Product #123 *(Illustration #8 and #9).*

Look at how reality unfolded, and compare the Week 1 - *Original Plan* with the *Actual Performance Week 1 - Week 5.*

Many businesses run operations on a monthly calendar, where two months in a row defines a trend. These businesses get into huge trouble before they know there is a problem. In the example *(Weeks 1 – 5),* a company that executes in monthly time frames would have started working on the problem in Week 8 and would have had a lot more unit volume to make up. A quarter is only three months *(or 13 weeks)* in length. In our example, the problem was realized and solved by Week 9. A weekly frequency is required to make quick, small, proactive adjustments versus large reactive ones, because reality can change the picture very quickly.

Let's compare the two:

Illustration #8 -

Picture of Product #123, Week 1 – Original Plan

Product SKU #123	Week 1	Week 2	Week 3	Week 4	Week 5
Inventory	400	300	500	400	400
Sales Forecast	100	100	100	100	100
Production/Purchase	0	300	0	100	200
Weeks-on-Hand	4	3	5	4	4
Weeks-on-Hand Maximum	5	5	5	5	5
Weeks-on-Hand Minimum	3	3	3	3	3

Illustration #9 -

Actual Performance Week 1 - Week 5

Product SKU #123	Week 1	Week 2	Week 3	Week 4	Week 5
Inventory	400	350	450	250	150
Actual Sales	50	200	200	200	200
Production/Purchase	0	300	0	100	200
Weeks-on-Hand	2.75	1.75	2.25	1.25	0.75
Weeks-on-Hand Maximum	5	5	5	5	5
Weeks-on-Hand Minimum	3	3	3	3	3

As the weeks unfold, MTNA allows the business to see the problem clearly and manage the problem in a real-time coordinated way at the *"level that matters."* MTNA does not make the decisions; however, MTNA makes the business aware of when an adjustment is required to balance demand and supply. The business Leaders and the Teams apply experience, judgment, and risk profiles to all decisions. MTNA will expose all decisions made over time, because Leaders and the Teams have a weekly picture of what the world looked like the day the Leaders decided to make an adjustment.

"Out of Bounds" Conditions

In the example problem above (Weeks 1-5), the only line or variable that changed was the Sales Forecast line to reveal that Product #123 could have too much or too little inventory in future weeks due to actual sales exceeding or not exceeding expectations today. There are only two "Out of Bounds" conditions that the business needs to manage to balance demand and supply: having too much or too little inventory in the future. *A simple and executable approach!*

Having too much future inventory means that the business needs to decide when to push off or delay production to a later date or not make production or purchases to stay under the Weeks-on-Hand Maximum. A too much future inventory condition is all about correcting the demand problem in the marketplace.

Having too little future inventory requires the business to spend money and coordinate all departments to take the correct action before the product runs out of inventory and damages customer relationships and sales. A too little future inventory condition is about the manufacturing and purchasing departments pulling in and/or increasing supply to meet the demand in the marketplace. The too little future inventory condition also requires the Sales and Marketing departments to adjust and set proper expectations in the marketplace and shift demand where possible.

MTNA allows reality to unfold today, while it reveals an *"Out of Bounds"* condition in the future. Now the business can calmly decide what to do about the future which today's reality has changed. This method makes the Leaders and Teams in the business look forward in time and solve relevant problems with small adjustments versus reactive, chaotic, silo-driven large adjustments, too late.

Let me show you other business reasons that drive the MTNA Gameboard to have too much or too little future inventory while keeping all other variables constant.

Too Much Future Inventory Examples:

Saleable Inventory returned from customer:
The beginning inventory increases and thus the Weeks-on-Hand measure increases in future time periods.

Underselling the Product forecast:
Sales are undersold and the Weeks-on-Hand measure increases in future time periods.

Over Production/Purchasing:
Over producing or purchasing increase inventory on the MTNA Gameboard, and the Weeks-on-Hand measure increases in future time periods.

Too Little Future Inventory Examples:

Saleable Inventory is put on hold and is not saleable:
The beginning inventory decreases and thus the Weeks-on-Hand measure decreases in future time periods.

Overselling the Product forecast:
Sales are oversold and the Weeks-on-Hand measure decreases in future time periods.

Under Production/Purchasing:
Under producing or purchasing decreases inventory on the MTNA Gameboard, and the Weeks-on-Hand measure decreases in future time periods.

So far, I have given you very basic examples to illustrate how MTNA flows for one product SKU and how one line or variable changes. Allow me to take the complexity up one level, and let's start moving more than one variable simultaneously to simulate a real world problem.

"*Businesses need to get out of being predictable and become unpredictable.*"

. . . **Mark Payne**

Example MTNA Gameboard Problem #2
Moving multiple variables at one time.

Using Illustration #10 as the original plan, what would happen if a raw material quality issue were found in Product #123? One hundred units of the current inventory had to be placed on hold. The bad raw material was going to be used in Week 2 production, and now manufacturing can only make 100 units in Week 2. The marketplace has discovered the quality issue, and the word is spreading fast. The sales orders have dropped in half. *Does this sound more like the real world?*

Illustration #10

The MTNA Gameboard Week 1 - Plan

Product SKU #123	Week 1	Week 2	Week 3	Week 4	Week 5
Inventory	400	300	500	400	400
Sales Forecast	100	100	100	100	100
Production/ Purchase	0	300	0	100	200
Weeks-on-Hand	4	3	5	4	4
Weeks-on-Hand Maximum	5	5	5	5	5
Weeks-on-Hand Minimum	3	3	3	3	3

Weeks-On-Hand Graph:

Week 1	Week 2	Week 3	Week 4	Week 5

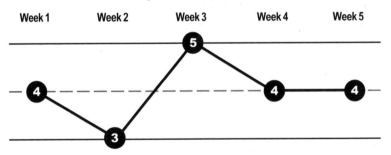

Let's see what the MTNA Gameboard would look like after we update and enter the reality about the bad raw material.

Here are the changes:

Finished goods inventory went down by 100 in Week 1. Sales were reduced by half for Weeks 1 – 5, and 200 units of production were lost in Week 2. All three lines in the MTNA Gameboard have changed.

How would you interpret Illustration #11?

Illustration #11 -

The MTNA Gameboard Week 1 - Bad Raw Material

Product SKU #123	Week 1	Week 2	Week 3	Week 4	Week 5
Inventory	300	250	300	250	300
Sales Forecast	50	50	50	50	50
Production/ Purchase	0	100	0	100	200
Weeks-on-Hand	6	5	6	5	6
Weeks-on-Hand Maximum	5	5	5	5	5
Weeks-on-Hand Minimum	3	3	3	3	3

Weeks-On-Hand Graph:

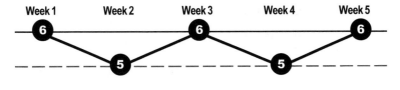

Is Product #123 out of bounds?

No.

Does the business need to pull in production and spend money to expedite new raw materials to catch the demand?

No.

Do you remember the examples in Chapter 1, *The Problem?* Most departments react to the bad news within their own set of data, systems, and spreadsheets. In this example, most companies would spend more dollars trying to replenish the 100 units of inventory on hold and the 100 units of Week 2 production lost. In this case, the demand is lost, and really, the product is in a potential too much future inventory problem if demand does not go back up to the 100 units per week level. This situation is not a "pull in production and expedite purchases at any costs" kind of problem. This is a "hold production and purchases where they are, and fix the quality issue in the eyes of the marketplace" kind of problem. The business must focus on driving demand back up to the 100 per week level.

What would have happened if the company pulled in production, replaced, manufactured and expedited the lost inventory, and demand continued at 50 units per week?

Answer: A lot of wasted money and effort would go down the drain.

MTNA allows all departments to view, participate, and solve business issues holistically. Departments can see the big picture and solve their piece of the problem at the same level without unknowingly working against each other and the business' profit line.

Multiple Products

There is another level of complexity to add to the MTNA Gameboard flow: ***How about more Products?*** In the previous examples, only one product has been displayed within the gameboard *(Product #123)*. How many companies sell just one product to the marketplace? Not many. MTNA is designed to manage tens of thousands of products simultaneously. This ability also adds a level of complexity because the business can trade demand and supply between products.

KEY INFO! **Cross-selling, trading raw material, or trading capacity gives the business more ways of working itself out of a problem.**

Multiple Product Example

Product #123 is underselling and Product #456 is overselling. These products are in the same product family; they have similar raw materials; and they use the same production line in the factory. So, you could lower sales and production for Product #123, and raise sales and production for Product #456. One pull in can be traded with one push out. Because the business is managing the change many weeks out in the future, manufacturing and suppliers will barely notice the change, and the business will continue to move forward in time.

MTNA Solves the Problem!

Now that you understand the mechanics, level, and flow of the MTNA Gameboard, let me expand your mind to solve the problems of plan alignment, lack of a common problem solving framework, and silo decisions that sub-optimize the business.

Let's add an organizational dimension to the MTNA Gameboard and then expand it into multiple organizational hierarchies.

Illustration #12

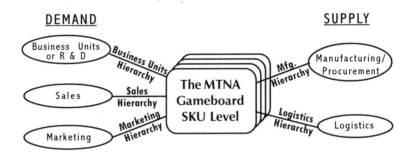

Roll up all of the SKUs for a particular business unit, factory, or warehouse, and show the MTNA Gameboard in their own product hierarchy. Roll up all of the SKUs for a particular sales region and show the MTNA Gameboard in their own geographical hierarchy.

Execute MTNA at a SKU level every week, and then roll up the SKU level data into different data hierarchies for each department or team.

The company can manage and execute the details at the bottom, and this time, the roll up of the future is real because the business is now running on one set of numbers and assumptions. If the roll up is short of expectations, then you head back to the MTNA Gameboard to solve the problem at the root. If any particular function were to suggest an action that would sub-optimize the balance, then an out of bounds condition will result.

Now we have created a game to be played by all departments in the business, which is . . . keep the MTNA Gameboard **in balance.**

Problems solved by MTNA

1. We now have plan and execution alignment across all departments continuously.
2. We have a common problem solving framework that adjusts to the reality of the marketplace. The Leadership is really viewing the true forward direction of the business, not some department's "spin" of the problem or gap.
3. Silo decisions that hurt the overall business are avoided because of the transparency of the information supplied by MTNA. Balancing the demand and supply equation becomes a cross-departmental game.

Now that you know how MTNA works, allow me to show you how to implement this proven methodology in the next chapter.

"Manage the details and then roll up the results. You cannot wish for results and force the details to match. It never works. You end up 'Chasing the Numbers' instead."

. . . Mark Payne

CHAPTER 3

Implementation of MTNA

The answer to the hint in the last chapter is to use your napkin! A cloth napkin is the only tool you will need to remove the cork. Now, how would you use the napkin to remove the cork? How would you implement your plan? Do you still believe this task is impossible? Keep thinking.

Even though I gave you a helpful hint on how to get the cork out, most people are still unable to solve the perplexing problem. Now you know how MTNA works; let's learn the steps on how to implement MTNA in your business.

Outline for MTNA implementation:

Step 1: Assess Business Model and Organization

Step 2: Organization: add a Sales & Operations Planning (S&OP) group and place them between demand and supply organizations

Step 3: Set up the MTNA Gameboard for all SKUs

Step 4: Educate both demand and supply organizations on how to use MTNA

Step 5: Implement the system that supports MTNA

Illustration #13 -

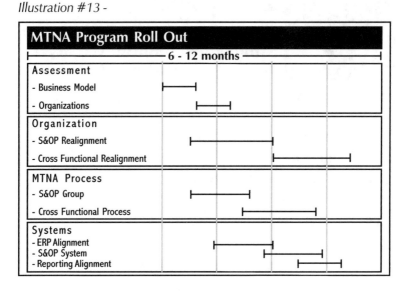

When implementing MTNA, it is not necessary to implement the process across the entire business. It can be used to run a division or section within the company. This flexibility would allow the implementers to work out the process before taking MTNA to the entire company. The process does require that the division or section own the inventory and sales forecasts across product SKUs. This requirement exists because the division implementing MTNA needs to have complete control over all future decisions.

Step 1:
Assessment of the Business Model and Organization

The first thing you must do to implement MTNA is to understand how the current business model operates at a SKU level. In my opinion, the best way to get this knowledge is to select a wide sample of SKUs and track them from the forecast process to delivery. As you map the path of the selected SKUs, note how each department manages the information around the set of SKUs you selected.

You will find the following:

1. SKU plans do not align with other departmental groups.
2. As reality unfolds in the marketplace, there is no cross departmental problem solving framework to adjust the SKUs. Adjustments are done at levels higher than SKUs (aggregation).
3. Departments manage the SKUs in isolation (silos), if they manage SKUs at all.

Does this sound familiar?
It should because it is the problem.

In step 1, you are simply taking an inventory of which groups and organizations talk to each other and solve problems at a SKU level. If you have large parts of the organization managing above the SKU level or not managing every SKU the company offers, quite frankly there is a lot of "overseeing" being done.

Another activity that needs to be understood is how a SKU's lifecycle is managed: A SKU is born and ramps up; a SKU is a steady seller; then, a SKU dies off and is replaced by another. How does your business manage the lifecycle process, and which organizations are involved? Remember, the MTNA Gameboard is operated for every SKU the company offers. If this process is loose or inefficient, the overall benefits of MTNA will be minimized.

The bottom line is that you understand how the organization is managing the SKU details of the business. When you implement MTNA, you will need to know how much change, effort, and focus are required to move all operational organizations to MTNA. We are simply defining the current business processes as Point A and MTNA as Point B.

Step 2: Organization
Add the Sales & Operations Planning Department

The second step in implementing MTNA is to create the **Sales & Operations Planning Department.** The person who leads this department needs to be selected. The person who is selected for this critical Leadership role must have experience in the *"demand side"* and *"supply side"* of the business. The person will be the facilitator of all the trade-offs between the two naturally opposing forces.

Another important trait that this newly appointed Leader must have is respect from the all the departments' Leaders within

Illustration #14 -

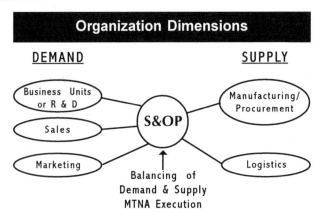

the company, divisions, or groups. As MTNA operates, the leader of the Sales & Operations Planning department must effectively facilitate trade-offs that might sub-optimize a particular group in order to maximize the entire company. This person must put the company first and have a balanced approach to solving all issues that MTNA reveals. The Sales & Operations Planning Leader is responsible for managing the process and maintaining integrity in the MTNA Gameboard.

After the company has selected this Leader, he or she will need to select their Team Members (i.e. Sales & Operations Planning Analysts). The job of these analysts is to maintain, manage, and update the MTNA Gameboard by product on a daily basis *(or as required)*. The analyst will derive the sales forecast and then input the Production/Purchase line in units by product SKU in 104 weekly time frames into the MTNA Gameboard. Every week, the analyst will need to gather the beginning inventory by product and update the Production/ Purchase line.

Because the MTNA Gameboard runs at the *"level that matters,"* the Sales & Operations Planning Leader must assign product SKUs to the analysts. Typically, an analyst can manage 300-400 product SKUs at one time. That number might seem high to some, so let me explain the workload.

Let's say an analyst is responsible for managing 400 product SKUs that the company offers to the marketplace. Assuming the Weeks-on Hand Maximums and Minimums are set in the correct place, as reality unfolds every week, the MTNA

Gameboard will typically reveal 20% *(80 SKUs)* of the products to have too much future inventory and 20% *(80 SKUs)* of the products have too little future inventory. Because the MTNA Gameboard is proactive and forward looking, only a small percentage *(about 10% or 8 SKUs)* of the too little future inventory type condition will need to be handled right away and pulled in and expedited. The rest of the too little and all of the too much types are execution adjustments that can be made in future weeks to balance the MTNA Gameboard. The number of analysts that are required to operate and manage the details of the MTNA Gameboard is determined by the number of product SKUs the company, division, or section offers the marketplace.

One mental note about the analysts - they become the most educated people in your business. They will know all of the details and get experience viewing all of the decisions and trade-offs at the *"level that matters."* I have found that Sales & Operations Planning Analysts who have run the process have great potential to run any department in the business. MTNA is a phenomenal training ground.

Good analysts already exist in your business today, as well as, Production Planners and Sales Forecasters. Gather them up and plug them into MTNA.

NOTE: MTNA S&OP Department does not do traditional S&OP activity. I am placing the S&OP group between the demand and supply organizations of the entire business to maintain the integrity of MTNA. Many companies have monthly S&OP meetings to look at a series of charts and grids of aggregated data. There is usually a lot more discussion around sales than around operations. Then, when a gap to plan arises, the root cause to the problem always requires more drilling through additional spreadsheets and systems.

Some people might say that MTNA is just a tactical process with little strategic value. This is absolute nonsense. Looking at aggregated information that is not actually reconciled to forward execution does not make it strategic. Aggregated information that is not actually reconciled to forward execution makes for an interesting discussion about hypothetical realities - *a complete waste of time.* Making strategic trades from an MTNA roll up is a strategy capable of being executed.

Step 3:
Set-Up the MTNA Gameboard

After the Sales & Operations Planning department is established and the entire product portfolio of SKUs is assigned to the analysts, the department must set up the MTNA Gameboard to represent the business model by product SKU. The Weeks-on-Hand Maximum and Minimum are **the keys to driving the business model by product SKU.**

Because every business has a different supply chain associated with their product portfolios, I will describe the basic, quick method to get the Weeks-on Hand section of the MTNA Gameboard implemented.

Illustration #15 -

Product Set-Up

Product SKU #123	Week 1	Week 2	Week 3	Week 4	Week 5
Inventory	400	300	500	400	400
Sales Forecast	100	100	100	100	100
Production/Purchase	0	300	0	100	200
Weeks-on-Hand	4	3	5	4	4
Weeks-on-Hand Maximum	6	6	6	6	6
Weeks-on-Hand Minimum	3	3	3	3	3

In the MTNA product set-up *(Illustration #15)*, the business builds inventory ahead of the sales order. When the customer orders the product, the product is immediately shipped to the customer. The Weeks-on-Hand Minimum is typically set by how often the product is produced or purchased. If a product is produced or purchased and placed into inventory every three weeks, then the Weeks-on-Hand Minimum would be three weeks. The Weeks-on-Hand Maximum would be set by multiplying the Weeks-on-Hand Minimum by two. This is a quick way to set up the Weeks-on-Hand measures for all products. As time moves forward, and the business and suppliers execute, the Operations Planning Leader and Analysts will start to adjust the Weeks-on Hand boundaries based on how the business and/or suppliers are executing by product SKU. These adjustments to the Weeks-on-Hand boundaries are typically made every three to six months.

Product Profiles:

- Hot Sellers
- Average
- Niche
- Discontinued

After the Sales & Operations Planning department has set up the MTNA Gameboard for every product SKU offered to the marketplace, the business must categorize every product SKU into four groups: Hot Sellers, Average, Niche, and Discontinued.

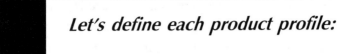

Let's define each product profile:

Hot Sellers:

These are products that the company makes and sells all the time. They are high volume products that the factory and suppliers love to make and the Sales force loves to sell. Typically, the top ten percent of your product portfolio fits this description.

Average:

These are products that the company makes and sells often. These are second tier products that the factory and suppliers make at least once a month. The Sales department meets an average need in the market place. Typically, sixty percent of the product portfolio will fit this profile.

Niche:

These are products that the company makes and sells to meet a special need or niche in the marketplace. The production, purchases, and sales are erratic and unpredictable because the sales volume is not high in any given week. Typically, twenty percent of the product portfolio will fit this profile.

Discontinued:

These are products that need to be discontinued. These are products that are in the current portfolio that have inventory, but have very little sales activity. Typically, the bottom ten percent of the product portfolio will fit this profile.

Take these product groups and manage them differently within the MTNA Gameboard. Keep the Hot Sellers as close to the Weeks-on-Hand Minimum as possible all the time. All departments should work together in order to achieve this goal. This practice will lower overall inventory and increase your inventory turns across the entire business. Manage the risk profile closely, because if you end up with too little future inventory, the business must react quickly to avoid stocking out. Manage the Average Products within the MTNA structure. There is no need to over manage Average Products. For Niche Products, set the Weeks-on-Hand Minimum and Maximum a few weeks higher than normal. Due to the high variance against forecasted sales and production/purchases, most customer dissatisfaction comes from the business not being able to deliver this type of product. Because Niche Products typically do not make up a lot of costs and inventory dollars, you can keep Niche Products higher in the Weeks-on-Hand range without costing the company a lot of cash.

KEY INFO!

If the business combines the strategies by product profile for Hot Sellers and Niche Products, you can lower the company's overall inventory while simultaneously raising customer service levels.

Every Three to Six Months:
Revise the Weeks-on-Hand Measures

The Sales & Operations Planning Leader will need to adjust the Weeks-on-Hand Minimums and Maximums by product SKU every three to six months. As the analysts get a feel for how each product SKU is performing, they should report which product's inventory to reduce without much risk. The Operations Planning Analysts will also provide guidance on which SKUs the business must continue to pull in and expedite production. The analysts will see obvious patterns develop when they see specific SKUs repeatedly go *"out of bounds"* with either too much or too little future inventory. Both of these pattern types need to be adjusted every three to six months or whenever necessary.

Step 4:
Educate All Departments on the Rules of the MTNA Gameboard.

After the Sales & Operations Planning department is positioned, and the MTNA Gameboard is set up for every product the company offers, it is time to train the other departments *(Leaders and Teams)* on the rules of MTNA. Use this time to build a new common language between departments to better serve the entire business. Explain how each department controls its section of the process and enlighten them on how much data visibility they will have. Every department will have visibility to see the effect it has on other departments by updating the MTNA Gameboard. Teach all departments how to implement and participate successfully using the MTNA Gameboard.

MTNA Gameboard by Department

Now that you have a feel for the flow of the MTNA Gameboard, let me introduce you to the Teams and their responsibilities in regard to the process. Keep in mind that not all departments in a business are listed *(although they might participate in certain decisions)* and that each department typically has more day-to-day responsibilities than what is listed.

Illustration #16 -

The Teams of The MTNA Gameboard

Sales & Operations Planning Department

This department becomes the "cross-departmental decision clearing house" for the entire company. The Sales & Operations Planning department will be required to update the beginning inventory on a weekly basis. The Sales Forecast lines and the Production/Purchase lines are typically updated weekly but can be updated less frequently if the business model allows.

The ***Sales & Operations Planning Leader*** will:

- ✦ Hold weekly meetings for all department Leaders and Teams to balance the business. This cross-departmental meeting actually runs the day-to-day operations of the company.
- ✦ Hold monthly meetings for all Leadership to view how the business is progressing through time. Leadership would approve any large trade-offs or apply resources when necessary.
- ✦ Ensure participation by Leaders and all departments as needed.
- ✦ Review results against projected measurements.
- ✦ Identify gaps and deviations.
- ✦ Resolve issues that have caused *"out of bounds"* conditions from the targeted performance goals.
- ✦ Modify and update the MTNA Gameboard for all departments weekly.

The Sales & Operations Planning department is responsible for managing the MTNA Gameboard and the integrity of the gameboard by SKU by week. The Sales & Operations Planning group will derive the sales forecast by SKU by week and then manage the Production/Purchase line within the MTNA Gameboard.

Marketing Department:

Responsible for managing the current product portfolio of the MTNA Gameboard and the sales forecast of new products. As a product begins to sell at a consistent pace, the Sales & Operations Planning Analysts will assume the product forecasting responsibility.

Sales Department:

Responsible for executing the Sales Forecast line within the MTNA Gameboard. Sales will also need to approve the sales forecast that the Operations Planning Analysts derive. The Sales & Operations Planning group will work with the Sales teams on a regular basis. The reason I like the analyst to do the detailed product SKU forecast is to reduce the administration burden on the Sales force. Let Sales adjust and approve the forecast, **not create the forecast.** Sales people need to do more selling and less administrative work.

Manufacturing Department:

Responsible for the Production/Purchase line within the MTNA Gameboard. Manufacturing must drive the Production/Purchase line to keep the Weeks-on-Hand within the Weeks-on-Hand Minimum and Maximum boundaries.

Procurement Department:

Responsible for the Production/Purchase line within the MTNA Gameboard. Responsible for supporting the production schedule with raw materials to meet the production line plan, or in a buy/sell relationship, support the Production/Purchase line in the form of a purchase to keep the Weeks-on-Hand within the Weeks-on-Hand Minimum and Maximum boundaries.

Finance Department:

Responsible for understanding all the financial trade-offs and interacting with all departments. All possible decisions and actions that the MTNA Gameboard has revealed must be understood and approved by the Finance Department.

Leadership:

Responsible for making final decisions that support the process with proper resources to carry out the execution phase of each decision (*i.e. approvals and funding*).

Employees become well rounded when they can see the "big picture." They escape from their silo and broaden their understanding of how the business works as a whole.

Below in illustration #17 are each department's direct responsibilities by MTNA Gameboard measures.

Illustration #17 -

Department's Responsibility
by MTNA Gameboard measures:

Product offering by SKU .... Marketing

Inventory .... Logistics/All

Sales Forecast .... Sales & Operations Planning Analyst / Sales Group

Production/Purchase .... Manufacturing and Purchasing

Weeks-on-Hand .... All Departments and Leadership

Weeks-on-Hand Maximum .... Sales & Operations Planning Leader

Weeks-on-Hand Minimum .... Sales & Operations Planning Leader

The MTNA Gameboard is all about people working with people using the same set of information. The MTNA Gameboard causes a natural check and balance of power and control. As the business implements and runs the process by product SKU and by week, all pieces of data are on the table and visible. All information is forward looking, and the future demand and supply picture is either in balance or *"out of bounds."* You will need to implement together and implement smart. The better your business executes MTNA, the more fun you will have and the more profit you will make.

Update and Inform the Leadership

The MTNA Gameboard repeats itself every week. The business will become more focused and execute better every week that passes. Every week the Sales & Operations Planning department needs to update the MTNA Gameboard. Remember, the forecast line is a guide that sets future production and purchases. The MTNA Gameboard helps the business to not rely solely on a sales forecast to execute supply activity. The MTNA Gameboard splits demand and supply and allows the business to manage the two lines independently. In other words, let the market and sales forecast move every week, but hold the Production/Purchasing line steady to allow the factories and suppliers to execute predictably. The MTNA Gameboard allows reality to reveal itself today so the business can make small adjustments for the future.

A good time to meet with the Leadership is after the MTNA Gameboards have been updated for every SKU. The Sales & Operations Planning Leader will need to update the business monthly on progress made, and how the departments are working together to solve issues that the market throws at the business every day.

Step 5:
Implement a System that Supports MTNA

With the organization and process defined and in place, the last step in the transformation is the implementation of a system that supports MTNA.

From a systems point of view, the biggest mistake I see organizations make is trying to manage the intersection of the demand plan, production plan, inventory plan and finance plan in Excel. While Excel is certainly a valuable tool in its own right, it simply is not capable of managing the MTNA Gameboard. To enable the entire business to run on a single set of numbers on a forward basis, there must be a system of record that all departments can rely upon. You need a single, forward-looking view of the business at all levels. Spreadsheets run by individuals in multiple departments cannot be reconciled to one set of numbers for the business. In addition to not providing a consistent decision-making framework, spreadsheets allow for individual manipulation and judgment of the data, which injects hidden *"taints"* into the numbers themselves. And, it is nearly impossible to roll up the data into the plethora of views required by the various execution centers of the business. By the time the Leadership views the numbers, no one is really sure where they came from. I am sure you have gone to a meeting and have asked the common question, *"Where did these numbers come from?"* Or you have made this statement, *"These numbers don't look right!"*

The second mistake I see organizations commonly make is

actually an extension of the first; they try to manage the business through a combination of Excel and the underlying ERP systems. ERP systems are designed for transactional execution and should be used for that purpose. A typical ERP implementation actually magnifies the problem because of how these systems were designed to flow a demand signal back through the supply chain.

MTNA is a process designed to manage the business at the *"level that matters"* and then roll up the forward view up for the various departments of the business. Every execution center (e.g., Sales, Marketing, Manufacturing, Logistics, Finance, etc.), needs to be able to see the information in a way that makes sense to them. Finance needs to see dollars and quarters; manufacturing needs to see units and weeks; logistics needs to see units and distribution centers, and so on. The business needs must drive the system design. Based upon my own experience, I have defined the following as the ideal capabilities for a system supporting MTNA:

- Ability to model the business on a forward basis, at the *"level that matters,"* and support the MTNA decision-making process
- Ability to roll the MTNA Gameboard up in multiple ways, on demand, to deliver the unique, contextual views required by each of the participants in the process
- Capable of interacting with multiple source systems for both acquiring data as well as pushing decisions back into the ERP system for execution
- Capable of running what-if scenarios, on demand, at both the *"level that matters"* as well as any level of aggregation

There are many systems suppliers providing solutions in and around the S&OP space, with pros and cons to each. Personally, I have used a solution offered by Symphony-Metreo Corporation, because the solution can be configured to support the entire MTNA process at scale. The system implementation time is around 12 weeks. Regardless of which vendor you choose, make sure you get a system that is capable of supporting and unlocking the value of the MTNA. Because once your business is truly running on a single set of forward numbers, from top to bottom, you will have transformed your business into a proactive enterprise that can "Make the Numbers."

WARNING:

If you implement the MTNA Gameboard, sit on your hands and refuse to make decisions, you will remain in a chaotic, reactive state. Proactively decide, and back up the decisions with resources and action. It is better for us to try and fail than to let the business run over us.

"If you make something you shouldn't, that's called obsolescence. If you don't make something you should, that's called a stock-out. Both cost you a lot of money."

. . . Mark Payne

Benefits of MTNA

In the last Chapter, I gave you the answer to the tool required to solve the cork in the wine bottle problem. Could your mind come up with the answer? Could your mind determine the benefit that the cloth napkin brought to the table? I will be honest with you; I had the napkin in my hand, but I didn't know what to do with it. I looked at the bottle and I looked at the cork, and my brain told me I needed to either enlarge the opening on the bottle or shrink the cork. I had no idea what value the cloth napkin brought to the equation. The trick and technique needed to be revealed. I was stumped.

In this book, I have defined the problem, recommended a solution called MTNA, and shown you how to implement MTNA in a business. The cloth napkin is in your hand. Can your mind come up with the results and benefits that MTNA brings to a business? I am sure you have a few ideas.

Let me outline the major benefits that MTNA brings to every business that implements it fully.

Results of MTNA:

1) Business is working off one set of operational numbers. Unit plan is already done. There is no need for each department to make up its own set of numbers and forecasts.

2) The production signal is managed and smoothed. Factories and suppliers get a smoother signal across time that increases their predictability and profitability.

3) Departments proactively balance the demand and supply picture.

Benefit #1
Business is Working Off One Set of Operational Numbers

The obvious benefit from using MTNA is that the business is working from one set of numbers. In *The Problem Chapter,* I described an environment that was not connected or aligned. The departments worked in silos and would react to reality independently. When the business adopts and implements MTNA, all departments have a common mission and framework to play together to solve the problems that the marketplace brings to the business every day.

Each department would use the *"one set"* of numbers that the MTNA Gameboard provides to reduce its own work load. Remember that we are rolling up the information from the

SKU level into different organizational dimensions to reflect the future direction of the business.

The major dimensions that any business would use are the following: Time, Product, Geography, and Measure.

Leadership would get a roll up of the future demand and supply picture for the entire company. If this roll up does not meet the original plan committed to the owners or shareholders, or a gap is revealed, then an adjustment can be implemented from the bottom-up because the Leadership is using MTNA. The Leadership is not relying on a department or person to interpret an aggregated view of the world. The Leadership team is viewing the details and the reality the business is currently executing via a rolled up result. The Leadership is no longer flying blind. They are now in tune with the business. Because the Leadership can see the true direction of the business continuously, problems are addressed quicker and decisions are made with precision because the root cause can be seen and understood. MTNA allows top-down management to drive bottom-up execution.

The Sales department has a tendency to use the MTNA Gameboard to reduce its workload by rolling up the future in the form of sales quotas. The MTNA Gameboard is showing the future sales units sold for every SKU every week for a two year timeframe. If you want to convert the units sold to a dollar quota, just apply the price times the units sold; then roll up the answer into a geography hierarchy. The geography hierarchy is built by adding all the SKUs sold in a particular sales region or geography.

The geography hierarchy would look something like this:

<u>Geography Hierarchy</u>

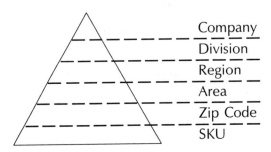

The sum of all the SKUs sold in a particular area could be used as a sales quota. Now your sales quota matches the true execution of the business.

Manufacturing and Procurement use MTNA to reduce their work load by rolling up the information by factory or supplier. The sum of all SKUs that a particular factory or supplier produce is rolled up to better manage the factory or supplier performance. Predictability against the Production/Purchase line within the MTNA Gamebaord is the most important performance measurement that Manufacturing and Procurement can manage.

The Logistics departments will roll up the sum of all SKUs that each logistic hub ships.

The Logistics Hierarchy would look something like this:

The Logistics Hierarchy

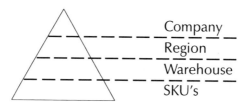

The Logistics team can monitor the performance of each warehouse and region that the SKUs are flowing through.

The Finance department gains many efficiencies using MTNA. The finance group no longer needs to forecast the unit and revenue direction for the business. This group can just pull the Sales Forecast line (in units) within the MTNA Gameboard and apply a price for every SKU, then roll up the dollar value for all of the SKUs. This is the true forward projected revenue plan that the company is selling against, and more importantly producing and buying against. The revenue plan is always done for two years out in time every week. The finance group will see this revenue plan fluctuate every week, because the MTNA Gameboard will allow reality to unfold today and adjust the future weeks to put the business back into a balanced state. Now the Finance group can pull the numbers every week and know the root cause for any variance.

No more aggregating results and drilling through multiple systems or spreadsheets to find the problems or the real numbers.

Working off one set of numbers reduces the friction in any cross-departmental meeting. Most of the time spent in a typical cross-departmental meeting is spent debating which group's numbers should be used.

The following questions and comments are always brought up in cross-departmental meetings:
- *What system did you pull those numbers out of?*
- *Whose spreadsheet are you using and where did you get your data?*
- *I don't believe your numbers. Use my spreadsheet.*
- *Our department does not recognize those numbers.*

How much time does a business waste *"Chasing the Numbers?"* More than you could ever imagine. Alignment can be achieved if you run MTNA. Your organization will make better, more informed decisions. How many top-down leadership decisions are made from numbers that are not tied to forward execution at the *"level that matters?"* The answer: all of them without the MTNA Gameboard.

Benefit #2
The Production Signal is Managed and Smoothed.

Another major benefit of MTNA is that the Sales Forecast line and Production/Purchase line are separated and managed independently. The production signal is managed and smoothed by MTNA. Factories and suppliers get a smoother signal across time that increases their predictability and profitability as well.

Let me explain. Most transactional systems in businesses today are set up to import a sales forecast, net out inventory safety stock and current orders, and then account for order-lead time and in-transit times. The sales forecast processes are usually on a monthly cycle, and the factory or supplier will see a dramatic change in the forecast that is being sent to them on a monthly basis. The reason the factories and suppliers see a dramatic change every month is that the sum of a month's forecast and order variances are all placed just outside the order lead time fence within the transaction system. The signal sent moves dramatically up or down every time a major sales forecast change is executed within the business. The factories and suppliers receive this forecast signal from the business and throw up their hands in disbelief.

The sales forecast received by the factories or suppliers looks like this over time.

Unmanaged and erratic.

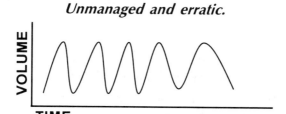

Talk about *"Chasing the Numbers!"* The factory and suppliers really do not know what number to chase because the numbers are changing regularly. The transactional systems throw the forecast over to the supply side of the business, and the supply side of the business must now efficiently run its assets while looking at numbers that move all over the place month-to-month.

So what do the factories do? How do you utilize a factory to run efficiently? You level-load the factory as much as possible to make the same quantities every week. Factories and suppliers want consistent volume week after week. The sales forecast is going up and down all of the time. So, the factories will *"judge"* the erratic forecast and then level-load the factory as much as they can. Then, the business complains about the unpredictable nature of the supply chain. This is why the demand side of the business calls the supply side of the business **UNPREDICTABLE.**

Talk to your suppliers and you will find that I am correct. From the factory or supplier perspective, the forecast that the business sends to them is a highly fluctuating number that makes no logical sense. The factory or supplier is not going to lose money, so they cover your needs the best that they can without losing money. The business ultimately pays for the under-utilization that the large variances in the sales forecast bring.

MTNA fixes this fluctuation problem by adjusting the Sales Forecast line in the MTNA Gameboard first. Then, on the Production/Purchase line below, the numbers are smoothed, worked independently and with sensitivity towards the objectives of the supply side of the business.

The MTNA Gameboard output of the production plan received by the factories or suppliers looks like this over time.

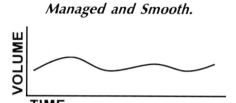

Managed and Smooth.

MTNA buffers the marketplace changes by using inventory to smooth the supply side of the business. As sales move up or down, the Production/Purchase line is managed separately to optimize the supply side of the business. The net effect to the business is better supply-side predictability and lower prices from the factories and suppliers.

Benefit #3
Departments will work together to proactively balance the demand and supply picture.

Most businesses stay in a reactive state when it comes to managing demand and supply issues. Departments tend to use one element of information, and the problem is not entirely seen or understood.

Let me give you a real world example.
The Sales team wants to know if the Supply Chain team will have enough inventories to cover the month. The Supply Chain team sends a file that has all of the available-to-sell inventory in the warehouse along with an aggregated number of inbound supplies for the month. What can the Sales team

do with this information? Basically, sell what is in stock.

What if the Sales & Operations Planning group sent the Sales team a MTNA Gameboard picture of all SKUs over the Weeks-on-Hand Maximum and all SKUs under the Weeks-on-Hand Minimum? The Sales team would receive a specific product list to push due to future high stock levels and a specific product list to avoid pushing due to future low stock levels. Then Sales would have the full future demand and supply picture to manage, not a partial picture to make assumptions from.

When you look at the MTNA Gameboard, you will see the future demand and supply flow presented for every SKU offered to the marketplace. Each SKU will have an upper and lower control limit to define the inventory thresholds. The objective of the game is to keep all SKUs offered to the marketplace in balance. If you believe having too much inventory is a bad thing and having too little inventory is a bad thing... *there is only one place to be...* **In Balance!**

The MTNA Gameboard allows reality to unfold today; then future time periods either go *"out of bounds"* high or low, and demand and supply decisions are made to correct the trend out in time. This reality creates a proactive organization. A framework and common objective exist to solve the projected problems of the business. All departments learn to stay ahead of the business and proactively solve problems that the MTNA Gameboard reveals in the future time periods. Departments learn how to *"Make the Numbers."*

Other Benefits of MTNA

▸ Flat Organizational Structure

MTNA can be run with a flat organization structure. A significant benefit to implementing MTNA is a flatter, more efficient organization that manages demand and supply activity. How many organization levels do you have in your company today? How many departments oversee the activity of another department? How many groups work outside the *"level that matters?"* MTNA allows the implementers to clearly see who is adding value to the business and who is not. MTNA creates a new paradigm for the business to restructure its organization.

▸ Employees Get an Education

Over time, MTNA teaches the employees how to handle the cause and effect relationship to any *"out of bounds"* condition that MTNA reveals. After adjusting to all types of problems over and over, the employees learn how to work through problems faster than before. Before long, the business is adjusting with ease and control to anything that the market-place throws its way. MTNA effectively teaches employees to efficiently manage risk.

MTNA will also train the Leaders and Teams to have a cross-departmental perspective. As the employees become experienced at balancing and managing the future demand and supply picture, they will see how their decisions affect the entire business. All departments will learn to view, participate, and solve business problems holistically.

▶ Better Decisions

MTNA increases the speed of decisions and expands the cross-departmental decision-making capacity of the business. Proactive control without panic will make the business efficiently adjust to reality. Another positive outcome to proactive decisions based on reality today is that your business will become unpredictable to your competitors since the business is not repeating the same decision patterns across time.

By logging the decisions over time, not only is the business creating an accountable environment, but also employees are learning not to make the same mistakes they have made in the past. The employees will make new mistakes, and the employees will learn from those mistakes, too.

▶ Dollars and Efficiencies

In my experience, these are the dollars that MTNA creates in a SKU driven volume business. The following results were felt in business sizes ranging from $500 million to $12 Billion, vertical models and outsourced models, 1,000 SKUs to 15,000 SKUs. These are the numbers that matter!

From a P&L perspective you can expect to see the following positive variances.

Revenue: + 1% to 2% - This positive effect is due to reducing stock-outs, setting realistic customer expectations, improving order fill rates, and providing better predictability to your customers.

COGS: -5% to -10% - This positive effect is due to the smoothing affect to the supply chain. Expediting costs drop dramatically. The supply chain that supports your business can utilize their assets more efficiently. If you simplify the SKU offering, you can get to the higher end of this range, because the factories will not need to change over as much. Reducing complexity reduces costs - always.

Operating Expense: -5%-10% - Simply stated, you do not need all the people you have in your business today. MTNA reduces redundancy that multiple sets of numbers create.

From a Balance Sheet perspective you can expect to see the inventory decrease by 20% to 40%. These numbers are achieved because every SKU that the company offers is actually managed and modeled independently. We are not throwing the SKU through some ERP black box methodology to be netted, twisted, and time-fence manipulated. An accountable human being is watching every move a SKU makes via the MTNA Gameboard and is providing a realistic production signal back through the supply chain.

If MTNA is running within your current business, acquiring and merging a new portfolio of products becomes very quick and easy. For example, you could buy a company and keep their customers and supply chain. Then, merge the acquired company's product portfolio into MTNA and discard the rest of the business. MTNA is an efficient concept because all areas of the business that manage demand and supply outside of the *"level that matters"* become unnecessary.

▶ Simple and Scalable

MTNA is simple to teach, inexpensive to implement, and is scalable to any size business. The MTNA Gameboard is designed to manage a large portfolio of products, or it can be adapted to run a section of the company. MTNA also allows your business to avoid needless mistakes by exposing all decisions made over time to facilitate a balanced approach to demand and supply management.

As the departments constantly make adjustments to the future based on reality today, decisions can be logged and archived to provide a *"look back"* on past judgments to see if the departments are making the right choices for the business. MTNA naturally exposes all forecasts and decisions over time. This fact creates an *"accountable environment."* MTNA requires the Leaders to constantly put the overall company's interest first.

MTNA has many benefits that will improve the efficiency of your business. The real question is how inefficient is your business today? Ironically, the more **inefficient** your business, the more MTNA will save your business in real dollars.

"MTNA is designed to allow a business to continuously plan, decide, and adjust the future demand and supply activity in order to maximize profit potential."

. . . Mark Payne

Conclusion

In Chapter 1, I asked you to force a cork into an empty wine bottle and then remove the cork without damaging the bottle or the cork. I started each Chapter of this book with the *"wine bottle"* analogy to take you through the learning process. I wanted you to experience a tough problem and show you a solution you had never seen before. I wanted to reveal a new way to look at and manage your business - ***A new way to use a cloth napkin!**** Fold the napkin in a point, and slide the pointed end into the bottle about 4 inches past the neck. Hold the bottle horizontally and flip the cork onto the napkin. This might take a few tries. Once the cork is on top of the napkin, pull the cloth napkin out slowly until half the cork is tightly wedged against the bottle and the other half of the cork is pressing against the napkin. Remember to hold the bottle horizontally. *Pull.* You will find that the cork is easier to pull out than it was to push in with your fingers. *Now you know.*

In business, we push the cork into the bottle every day. We typically do not work with each other to optimize the business because there is not a common process for us to rally around. MTNA is a methodology that can be applied to solve the dysfunctional way most businesses behave. There is a different way to run the business that allows all departments to work together for the common good of the enterprise. We just need to open our minds to a new way, organize differently, and play a different game. *Now you know.*

EPILOGUE

By now you have probably polished off a bottle of wine, pushed the cork into the empty bottle and grabbed a cloth napkin. It works. My objective of this book was to show you a new way to change your business into a more efficient enterprise. A new concept. I did not want to write a formal textbook with formulas and heavy math to reveal a statistical concept. I wrote this book for the business person, and I wanted the audience to be able to understand MTNA in a business context. MTNA is built to support a business. For the statisticians, mathematicians and PhDs... *this epilogue is for you.*

I created a business process that balances the demand and supply issues by using a forward looking weeks-on-hand calculation and applying an upper and lower control limit to every SKU the company offers; thus, managing and controlling the demand and supply flow for the entire company. I take the results from every forward looking weeks-on-hand equation and roll up the measures into different hierarchies to serve each area of the business. Although each area of the business looks at the world differently, the company is now working off one set of numbers; therefore, driving redundant work and effort out of the company.

I then added a framework *(i.e. MTNA Gameboard)* to balance and execute the equation over time across all business departments. The end result is a business that works together toward a common goal, using one set of numbers... a business that **Makes the Numbers!**

. . . Mark Payne

INDEX

A

Accountable environment, 94
Annual business plan, 6, 7
Annual plan, 6, 7, 8
Annual planning process, 7
Average products, 67, 68, 69

B

Balance sheet, 93
Benefit #1:
  Business is working off one set of operational numbers, 82
Benefit #2:
  The production signal is managed and smooth, 86
Benefit #3:
  Departments will work together to proactively balance the demand and supply picture, 89
Better decisions, 92
Business plan, 18

C

Chase the numbers, 2, 5, 17, 18, 23
Chasing the numbers, 2, 86, 87

COGS, 93
Cork in the bottle scenario, 4, 5, 8, 17, 23, 25, 27, 59, 81, 97
Cross-departmental, 6, 28, 29
Cross-departmental decision making, 92
Cross-departmental meetings, 86
Cross-departmental problem solving framework, 5, 11, 23, 28, 61
Customer relationships, 22

D

Data hierarchies, 56
Demand and supply, 22, 27, 29, 31, 34, 48, 55, 57, 59, 62, 75, 76, 82, 83, 89, 90, 91, 94
Demand plan, 77
Departmental plan, 29, 31
Departmental reports, 30
Discontinued products, 67, 68
Dollars and efficiencies, 92

E

Employees get an education, 91
ERP, 78, 93
ERP systems, 78
Erratic forecast, 88

INDEX

Example MTNA Gameboard problem #1

One product over time, 35

Example MTNA Gameboard problem #2

Moving multiple variables at one time, 51

Excel spreadsheets *(Microsoft)*, 77, 78

F

Finance, 7, 15, 16, 19, 21, 74, 78, 85

Finance plan, 77

Flat organizational structure, 91

Forecast process, 61

G

Gameboard measurement set-up by product SKU by week, 31

Geographical hierarchy, 56

Geography, 83

Geography hierarchy, 30, 83, 84

H

Hot sellers *(products)*, 67, 68, 69

I

Illustration #1

Manage the details, roll up the results into multi-dimensions, 29

Illustration #2

The MTNA Gameboard, 32

Illustration #3

Product #123, week 1 - original plan, 36

Illustration #4

New picture of product #123, week 2, 37

Illustration #5

New picture of product #123, week 3, 39

Illustration #6

New picture of product #123, week 4, 41

Illustration #7

New picture of product #123, week 5, 44

Illustration #8

Picture of product #123, week 1 - original plan, 47

Illustration #9

Actual performance week 1 - week 5, 47

INDEX

Illustration #10
  The MTNA Gameboard week 1
  - plan, 52
Illustration #11
  The MTNA Gameboard week -
  bad raw material, 53
Illustration #12
  Multiple organizational
  hierarchies, 56
Illustration #13
  MTNA program roll out, 60
Illustration #14
  Organizational dimensions, 62
Illustration #15
  Product set-up, 66
Illustration #16
  The teams of the MTNA
  Gameboard, 71
Illustration #17
  Department's responsibility by
  MTNA Gameboard line item, 75
Inventory, 33
Inventory plan, 77

K

Key questions to ask about a SKU
  going "out of bounds" above
  the weeks-on-hand maximum,
  38

Key questions to ask about a SKU
  going "out of bounds" below
  the weeks-on-hand minimum,
  43

L

Leaders, 94
Leaders and teams, 91
Leadership, 7, 8, 14, 15, 17-20,
  30, 48, 49, 57, 62, 63, 70, 72,
  74, 76, 77, 83
Level that matters, 28, 30, 47,
  63, 64, 78, 86, 91, 93
Logistics, 78, 85
Logistics hierarchy, 85

M

Make the numbers, 2, 28, 29,
  79, 90
Make the numbers approach, 2,
  18
Make the numbers, don't chase
  the numbers, 1
Managed and smooth, 89
Manufacturing, 11-13, 15, 16,
  19-22, 30, 42, 45, 73, 78, 84
Market and sales forecast, 76

INDEX

Marketing, 6, 15, 16, 18-21, 49, 73, 78

Measure, 83

MTNA, 2, 3, 16, 18, 24, 27-31, 34, 35, 45, 47, 49, 50, 54-57, 59-64, 66, 69, 70, 75, 77-79, 81-83, 85-89, 91-94, 97

MTNA Gameboard, 28-31, 34, 38, 42, 29, 50, 52, 53, 55-57, 59, 61, 63-65, 67, 69-79, 82-86, 88-90, 93, 94

MTNA Gameboard by department, 71

MTNA measure definitions, 33

Multiple organizational hierarchies, 56

Multiple product example, 55

Multiple products, 55

N

Niche products, 67-69

O

Operating expense, 93

Operations planning analysts, 70, 73

Operations planning leader and analysts, 67

Out of bounds, 34, 38, 42, 45, 48, 49, 54, 57, 70, 72, 75, 90, 91

P

Problem #1

Plans don't align to other departmental groups, 6

Problem #2

Companies do not have a cross departmental problem solving framework to adjust to reality, 10

Problem #3

Departments are left to their own devises to "Chase the Numbers" from their "silo" perspective, 17

Problem solving framework, 11, 13, 17, 57

Procurement, 11-13, 15, 16, 19-22, 42, 84

Product, 83

Product hierarchy, 56

Product profiles, 67

Product SKU, 30, 31, 34, 35, 38, 42, 45, 50, 60, 63-65, 67, 70, 73, 75

Production, 6, 88

INDEX

Production line, 73, 84, 89

Production plan, 77, 89

Production planners, 64

Production/Purchase, 33, 45, 63, 72, 76, 86

Purchasing, 30

Q

Questions for your annual business planning process, 9

R

Revenue, 92

Revenue plan, 15, 85

S

S&OP, 65, 79

Sales, 6, 7, 11, 12, 15, 16, 19-21, 45, 49, 73, 78, 83, 89, 90

Sales & operations planning (S&OP), 59, 72, 73, 76

Sales & operations planning analysts, 63, 64, 73

Sales & operations planning department, 62, 63, 65, 67, 70, 72

Sales & operations planning leader, 63, 70, 72, 76

Sales forecast, 33, 34, 45, 48, 63, 72, 73, 76, 85-88

Sales forecasters, 64

Sales prevention departments, 21

Sales quota, 84

Sales region, 83

Sales team, 38

Silo, 22, 24

Silo decisions, 56, 57

Silo example #1

New product launch is delayed by five weeks, 18

Silo example #2

Product demand exceeds wildest expectations as demand rises 200% over the sales forecast this month, 20

Silo-based, 20

Silos, 17, 18, 23, 28, 61, 82

Simple and scalable, 94

SKUs, 56, 59-62, 65, 70, 72, 83-85, 90, 92, 93

Special products, 69

Spreadsheets, 77, 86

Step 1:

Assessment of the business model and organization, 60

INDEX

Step 2:

Organization; add the sales &
operations planning
department, 62

Step 3:

Set-up the MTNA Gameboard,
65

Step 4:

Educate all departments on the
rules of the MTNA Gameboard,
70

Step 5:

Implement a system that
supports MTNA, 77

Supply chain team, 89, 90

Symphony-Metreo Corporation,
79

Systems or spreadsheets, 86

T

Teams, 8, 14, 17, 20, 48, 49, 63,
70, 72

Time, 83

Time horizon, 33

Too little future inventory, 50,
64, 69, 70

Too little inventory, 48, 49, 90

Too much future inventory, 54,
64, 70

Too much inventory, 48, 90

U

Unmanaged and erratic, 87

Update and inform the
leadership, 76

W

Weeks-on-Hand, 33

Weeks-on-Hand Maximum and
Minimum, 34

INDEX

Quotes used in this book are
Copyright © 2007, all rights reserved, Mark Payne

"If you believe having too much inventory is a bad thing and having too little inventory is a bad thing ... there is only one place to be ... In Balance!" 26

"Don't be normal; be exceptional!" 35

"Businesses need to get out of being predictable and become unpredictable." 51

"Manage the details and then roll up the results. You cannot wish for results and force the details to match. It never works. You end up 'Chasing the Numbers' instead." 58

"Employees become well rounded when they can see the 'big picture.' They escape from their silo and broaden their understanding of how the business works as a whole." 74

"If you make something you shouldn't, that's called obsolescence. If you don't make something you should, that's called a stock-out. Both cost you a lot of money." 80

"MTNA is designed to allow a business to continuously plan, decide, and adjust the future demand and supply activity in order to maximize profit potential." 96

Order Form

MAIL ORDERS TO:
Make the Numbers™
9803 Spring Cypress Rd., Ste. 600-297
Houston, Texas 77070
EMAIL ORDERS: orders@MakeTheNumbers.com

Please send the following: "Make the Numbers, Don't Chase the Numbers"
by Mark Payne, ISBN: 978-0-97531-396-1, Penworth Publishing

_____ Total number of books
__X_____ Cost per book
($34.95 per book - see website for bulk pricing)
_____ Total dollar amount for books
_____ Tax* (8.25% for Texas)
_____ Amount for shipping and handling*
_____ Total amount enclosed

*SHIPPING: Free Shipping for Bulk Purchases (250 or more) when there is one
ship-to location.
*SHIPPING: U.S. (less than 249 books and/or shipped to multiple locations):
$3.99, 1st book, $1.00 ea. additional book
***SHIPPING: International (less than 249 books and/or shipped to multiple
locations):** $9.00, 1st book, $5.00 ea. additional book
*SALES TAX: Please add 8.25% for products shipped to Texas addresses.

PAYMENT BY: ☐   Check enclosed
                 ☐   Credit Card: ☐ Visa   ☐ MC   ☐ Amer. Exp.

Card No.: _____   Exp.: _____   Security Code: _____

Name on Card:_____

Please send more information about:
☐ Other Books/Products   ☐ Speaking/Seminar/Certification   ☐ Consulting

Name: _____

Country: _____

Address: _____

City: _____ State: _____ Zip: _____

Phone: _____ Email: _____

Make The Numbers™ ◆ Mark Payne
(281) 733-8097 ◆ 9803 Spring Cypress Rd., Ste. 600-297 ◆ Houston, TX 77070
www.MakeTheNumbers.com ◆ Email: Orders@MakeTheNumbers.com